The Joy of Wedding Music

**A Delightful, Up-To-Date Collection of Festive and Inspirational Selections,
Vocal and Instrumental, Baroque to Modern.
Compiled and arranged for piano, with words and chord names,
by Denes Agay.**

Cover Illustration by Janice Fried

This book Copyright © 1990 by Yorktown Music Press, Inc.,

Order No. YK 21533
US International Standard Book Number:0.8256.8080.8
UK International Standard Book Number:0.7119.2298.5

Exclusive Distributors:
Music Sales Corporation
225 Park Avenue South, New York, NY 10003
Music Sales Limited
8/9 Frith Street, London W1V 5TZ England
Music Sales Pty. Limited
120 Rothschild Street, Rosebery, Sydney, NSW 2018, Australia

Printed in the United States of America by
Vicks Lithograph and Printing Corporation

Yorktown Music Press, Inc.
New York/London/Sydney

CONTENTS

PRELUDES, INTERLUDES, AND TRADITIONAL VOCAL SOLOS

PROCESSIONALS

RECESSIONALS

MODERN LOVE SONGS

Editor's Note: Numerous selections are appropriate as both Processionals and Recessionals.

Joyful, Joyful We Adore Thee
from Ninth Symphony

Henry Van Dyke

Ludwig van Beethoven

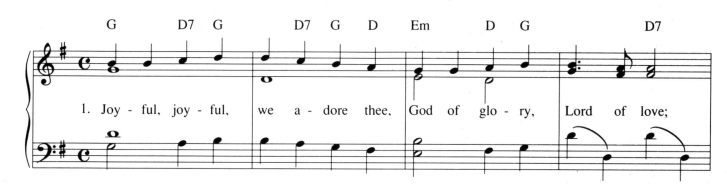

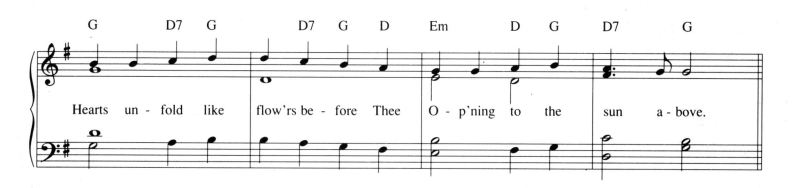

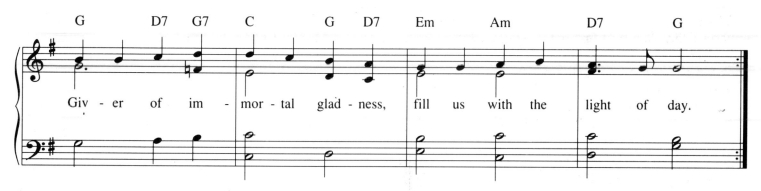

2. Mortals, join the happy chorus
Which the morning stars began;
Father love is reigning o'er us,
Brother love binds man to man.

Ever singing, march we onward,
Victors in the midst of strife,
Joyful music leads us sunward
In the triumph song of life.

Trumpet Tune

Henry Purcell

Air
from Water Music

George Frideric Handel

Slowly and solemnly

O Perfect Love

Dorothy F. Gurney

Sir Joseph Barnby

2. O perfect Life, be Thou their full assurance
   Of tender charity and steadfast faith,
   Of patient hope, and quiet, brave endurance,
   With childlike trust that fears nor pain nor death.

3. Grant them the joy which brightens earthly sorrow;
   Grant them the peace which calms all earthly strife,
   And to life's day the glorious unknown morrow
   That dawns upon eternal love and life.

Praise My Soul the King of Heaven

Henry Francis Lyte

Sir John Goss

2. Praise Him for His grace and favor
   To our fathers in distress;
   Praise Him still the same as ever,
   Slow to chide, and swift to bless:
   Alleluia! Alleluia!
   Glorious in His faithfulness.

3. Angels in the height adore Him!
   Ye behold Him face to face;
   Saints triumphant bow before Him!
   Gathered in from every race.
   Alleluia! Alleluia!
   Praise with us the God of grace.

*This hymn was used as processional in the wedding of Princess
Elizabeth (now Queen Elizabeth) at Westminster Abbey, on November 27, 1947.*

Morning Has Broken

Gaelic melody

With quiet motion

2. Sweet the rain's new fall
   Sunlit from heaven,
   Like the first dew fall
   On the first grass.
   Praise for the sweetness
   Of the wet garden,
   Sprung in completeness
   Where his feet pass.

3. Mine is the sunlight,
   Mine is the morning,
   Born of the one light
   Eden saw play.
   Praise with elation,
   Praise every morning,
   God's recreation
   Of the new day!

Amazing Grace

Folk hymn

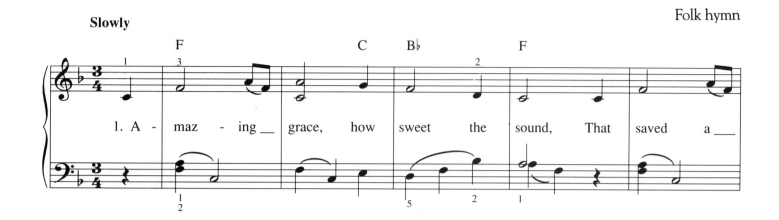

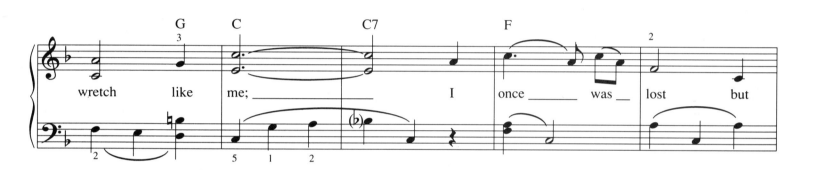

2. 'Twas grace that taught my heart to fear,
   And grace my fears relieved;
   How precious did that grace appear
   The hour I first believed.

3. Through many dangers toils and snares,
   I have already come;
   'Tis grace that brought me safe thus far,
   And grace will lead me home.

4. How sweet the name of Jesus sounds
   In a believer's ear;
   It soothes his sorrows, heals his wounds,
   And drives away his fear.

5. Must Jesus bear the cross alone
   And all the world go free?
   No, there's a cross for ev'ry one
   And there's a cross for me.

Bridal Chorus
from Lohengrin

Richard Wagner

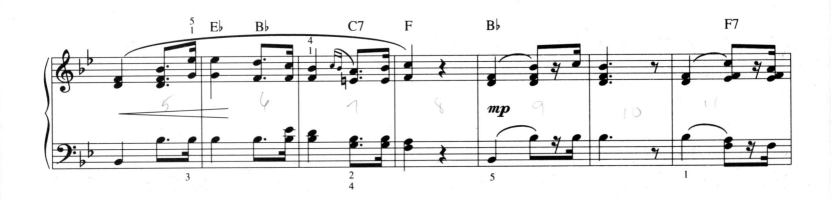

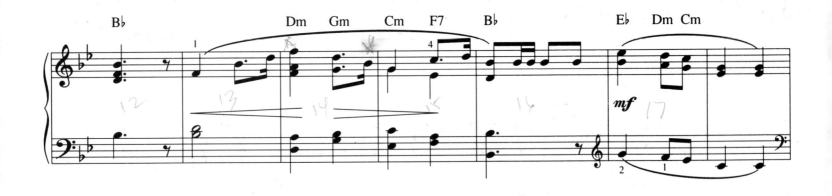

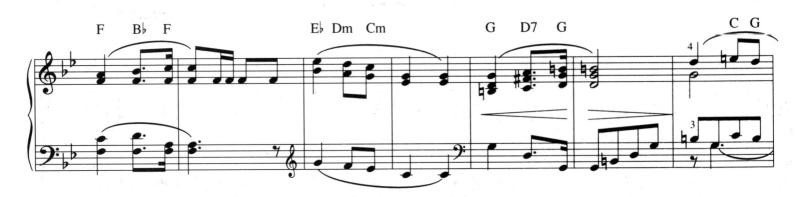

Trumpet Voluntary

Jeremiah Clark

Con moto maestoso

Fine

D.S. 𝄋 al Fine

Solemn Procession

Denes Agay

Slow, majestic walking tempo

Arioso

Johann Sebastian Bach

Andante moderato

Love Divine, All Loves Excelling

Charles Wesley

John Zundel

Sheep May Safely Graze

Johann Sebastian Bach

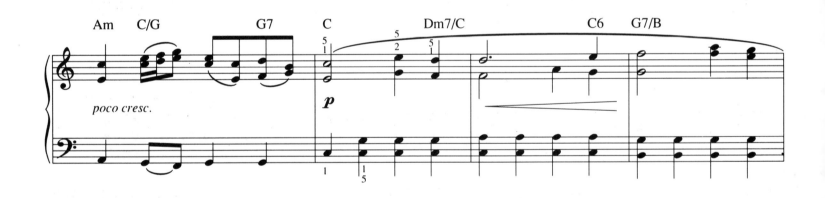

Ave Maria

Franz Schubert

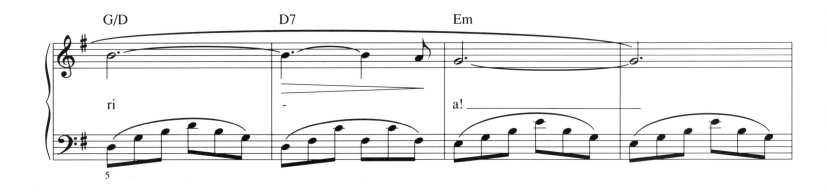

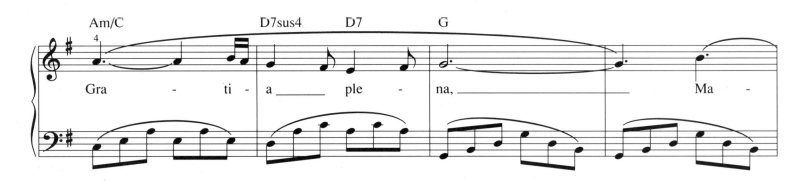

Jesu, Joy of Man's Desiring

Johann Sebastian Bach

Je - su, joy of man's de - sir - ing,
Drawn by Thee our souls as - pir - ing

Ho - ly wis - dom, Love _____ most
Soar to un - cre - a - ted

* ⊕ *Optional cut to coda*

Striv - ing still to truth un - known,

Soar - ing, dy - ing round ___ Thy ___

⊕ **Coda**

throne.

In the Garden
from Rustic Wedding Symphony

Karl Goldmark

I Love You Truly

Carrie Jacobs Bond

2. Ah! love, 'tis something to feel your kind hand,
   Ah! yes, 'tis something by your side to stand;
   Gone is the sorrow, gone doubt and fear,
   For I love you truly, truly, dear.

Because

Edward Teschemacher

Guy d'Hardelot

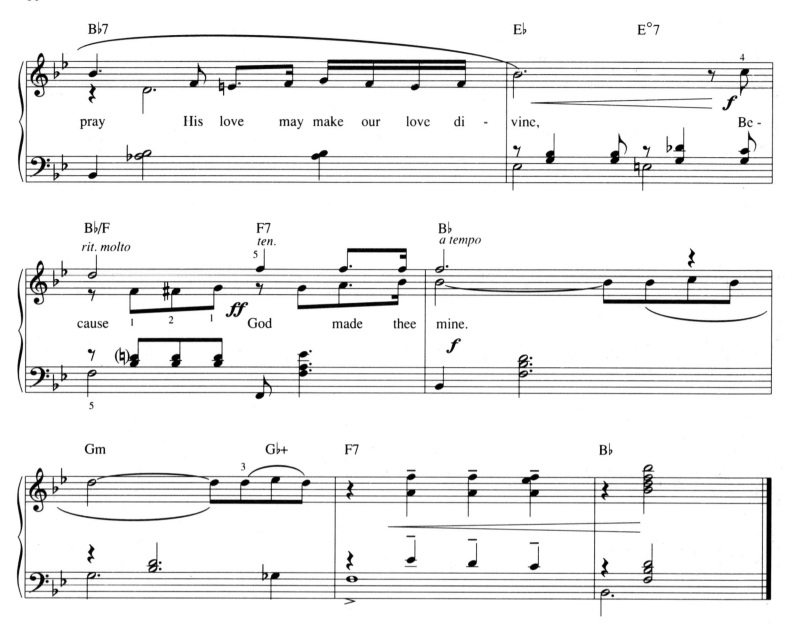

pray   His love   may make   our   love di - vine,   Be-

cause   God   made   thee   mine.

Baroque Fanfare

Jean Joseph Mouret

Moderato con moto

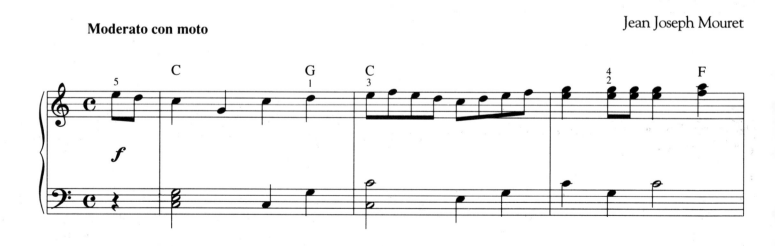

The Lord's Prayer

Matthew 6: 9–13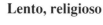

Albert Hay Malotte

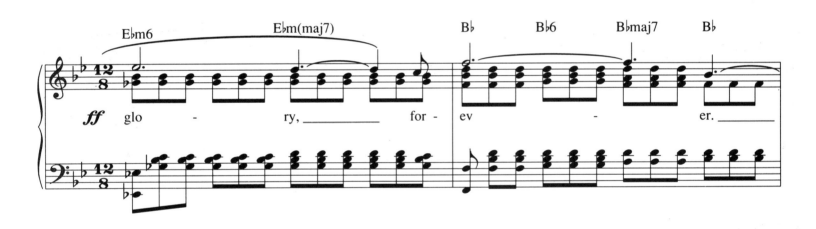

For You, My Love
(*solo or duet*)

Sidney Leif

Denes Agay

Moderately, freely moving

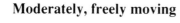
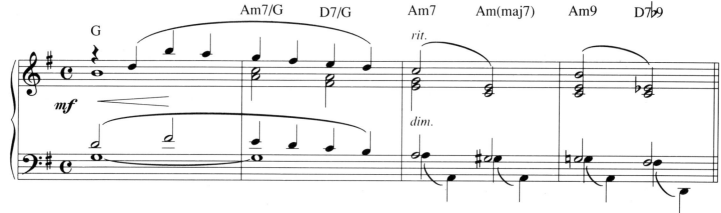

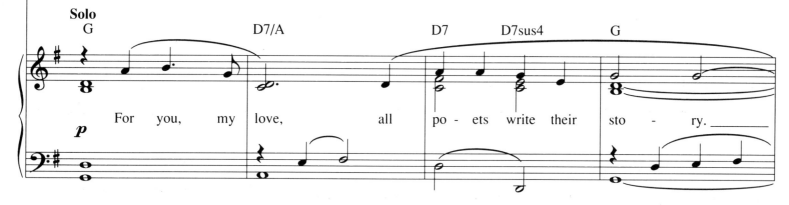

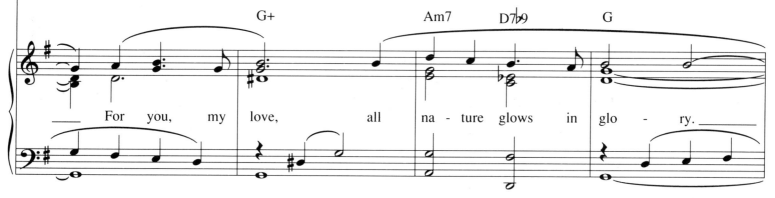

* Section between the signs (⊕) may be omitted.

Wedding Prayer

Fern Glasgow Dunlap

I Love You

Edvard Grieg

Dedication

Jean Reynolds Davis

Robert Schumann
Op. 21, no. 1

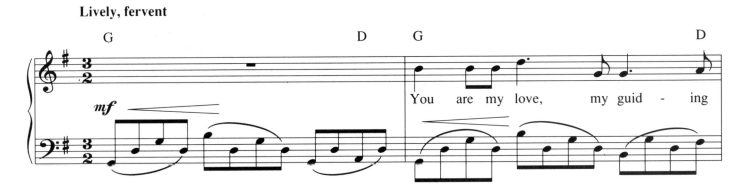

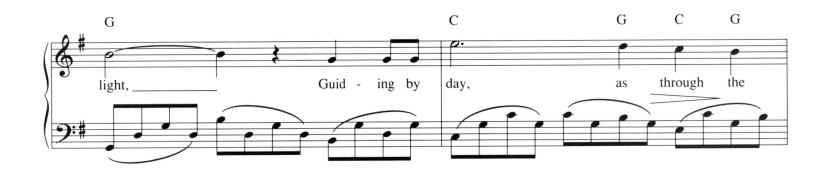

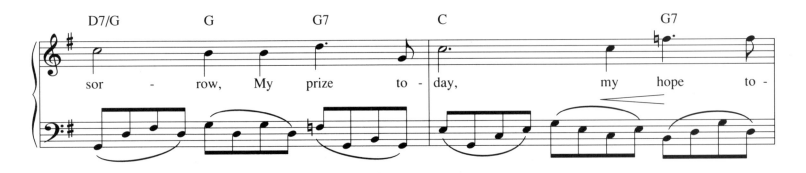

We've Only Just Begun

Words and Music by
Paul Williams and Roger Nichols

Somewhere

from West Side Story

Music by Leonard Bernstein
Words by Stephen Sondheim

for my daughter on her seventeenth birthday

Old Irish Blessing

Traditional

Denes Agay

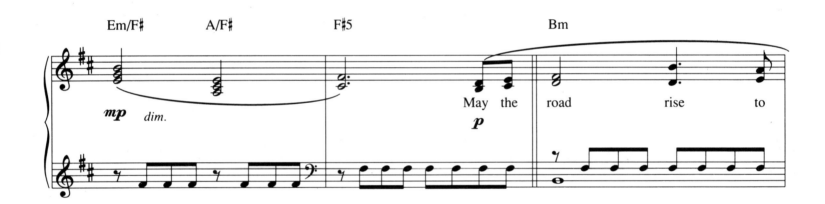

Bm A G A Bm A D Bm A G A
p
sun shine warm up - on your face, The rains fall sort ___ up -
Bm A Bm Em A Bm F♯7 Bm Em6
mp
on your fields, And un - til we meet a - gain, May
F♯ Em F♯ Bm G
mf f
God, may God, May God hold you
F♯m B G♯m
f
in the palm of his hand. May the Lord bless you and

One Hand—One Heart

from West Side Story

Music by Leonard Bernstein
Words by Stephen Sondheim

Slowly, tenderly

I Need You To Turn To

Words and Music by
Elton John and Bernie Taupin

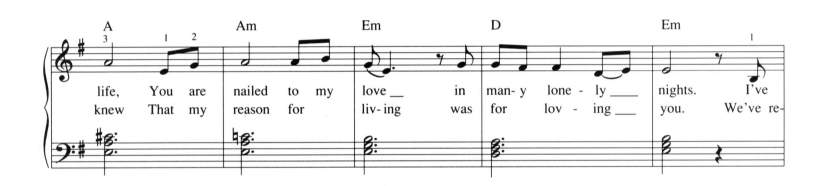

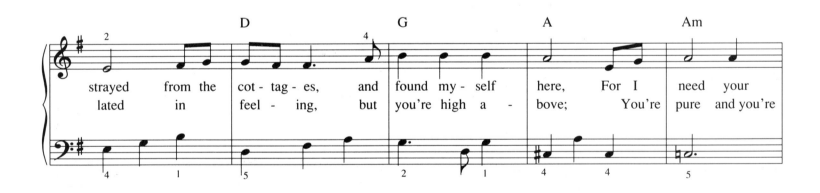

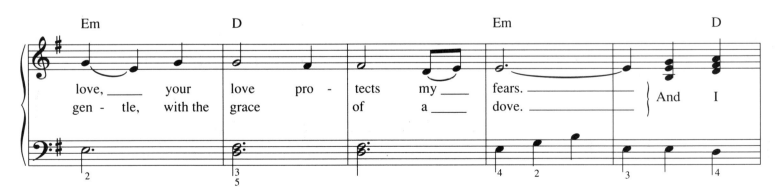

Bridge Over Troubled Water

Moderate, not too fast, like a spiritual

Words and Music by
Paul Simon

Since You've Asked

Words and Music by
Judy Collins

A Whiter Shade Of Pale

Words and Music by
Keith Reid and Gary Brooker

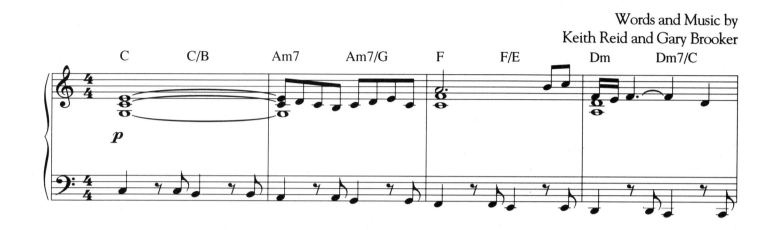

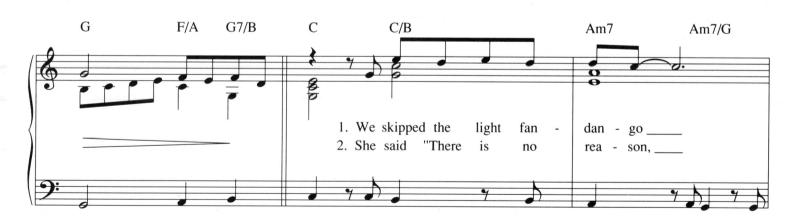

1. We skipped the light fan - dan - go
2. She said "There is no rea - son,

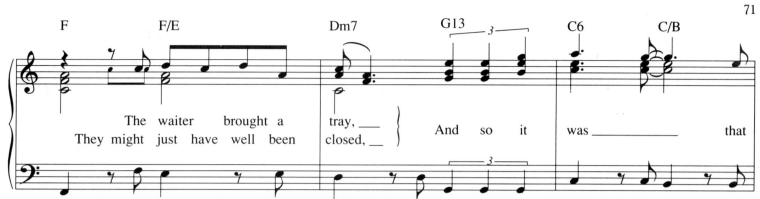

The waiter brought a tray, ___
They might just have well been closed, __
And so it was _____ that

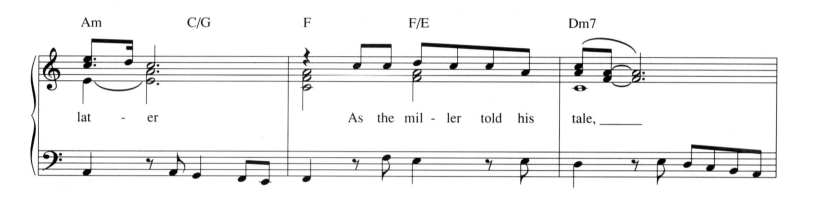

lat - er
As the mil - ler told his tale, _____

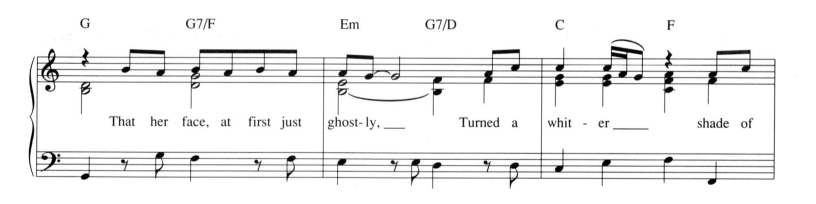

That her face, at first just ghost-ly, ___ Turned a whit - er _____ shade of

1.
pale. _____

2.
pale. _____

Wedding March
from A Midsummer Night's Dream

Felix Mendelssohn

Festival Rondo

Henry Purcell

Con moto maestoso

D.C. al fine

Canon

Johann Pachelbel

Lento moderato

Psalm XVIII

Benedetto Marcello

Con moto; maestoso

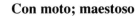

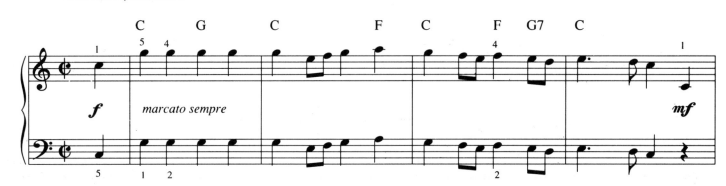

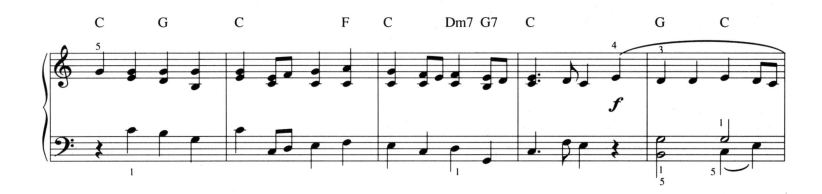

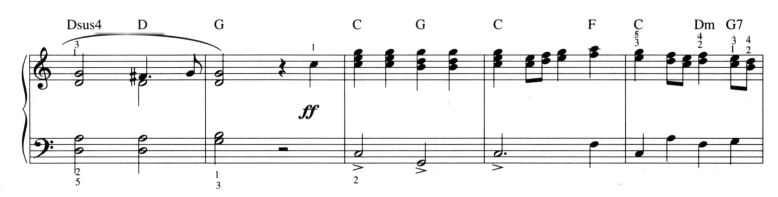

Now Thank We All Our God

Martin Rinkart

Johann Crüger